gives the reader a real look into the sense of fear, loss, determination, love and ultimately acceptance that every special needs mom goes through.

—Hartley Steiner, author of *This is Gabriel Making Sense of School* and *Sensational Journeys*

In using the simple phrase that "life has thrown me overboard" to describe the complexity of her son's challenges, Jennie's honest words convey a range of emotions that parents of special needs children will relate to very easily.

—Phillip Hain, Executive Director, Autism Speaks, Los Angeles Chapter

"You can do this," describes Jennie well, who speaks of her living story and writes to those of us who've participated with her in workshops and training sessions. It's not only the expression of words and affirmations, but her generosity of presence.

—Regina King, Poet

Autism
disrupted

...a mother's journey of hope

*With love,
gratitude and hope...*

Poems
by Jennie Chapman Linthorst

Autism
disrupted
...a mother's journey of hope

Jennie Chapman Linthorst

CardinalHouse
PUBLISHING

Chapman Linthorst, Jennie
Autism disrupted: A Mother's Journey of Hope / Jennie Chapman Linthorst
ISBN 978-0-9826472-1-9

For Graham, my greatest teacher.

Contents

Acknowledgements
Foreword by Ricki G. Robinson, M.D., M.P.H.

Acknowledgements

To my husband Erik, thank you for your love and support on this journey. Thank you to my father and sister for loving me through all these years. To my late mother, and grandmother, your voices are with me every day. To my teacher and editor, Stellasue Lee, you are a gift in my life as you continue to teach my voice to shine. To Dr. Ricki Robinson for being our expert guide on this continuing journey. To Dana Kae Bonahoom for your guidance with Graham, and your love and faith in me as a mother; and to all the therapists, teachers and doctors who have worked one on one with Graham. You are the angels in this miracle. Thank you to the programs at the Option Institute and the University of Santa Monica for encouraging and inspiring my self-growth. Thanks to Marie Teagardin, Steve Gaffney, Eric Hansen and the team at Cardinal House Publishing for the beautiful photography and book design. Thank you to Kathie Papera for your marketing expertise. And lastly, to all of my dear friends and family, I am forever in gratitude for your patience, love, and endless support.

FOREWORD
by Ricki G. Robinson, M.D., M.P.H.

As a pediatrician with twenty years of experience caring for children and families living with autism, I have been so privileged to join hundreds of families seeking help for their children with these types of behaviors. When parents hear the "A" word their worst fears are confirmed. I can see it in their eyes and body language as the cloud of uncertainty darkens their days and fear dashes their dreams for their child. Their lives and their families are forever changed in inexplicable ways.

This beautiful and courageous collection of poems is really a series of snapshot stories documenting the introspection, love, courage, resiliency and hope familiar to all parents of special children. Sometimes a poem is the only story a parent has the time to write, and in this case, we are all the richer.

Autism disrupted: A Mother's Journey of Hope, Jennie Linthorst's poignant chronicling of early motherhood evokes the emotional swings of her journey with her husband Erik and their son Graham once autism enters their life when Graham is nearly a year old.

Graham, an adorable blonde, blue-eyed toddler, exhibited many worrisome behaviors at our first visit. He was obsessively attracted to lines, which he crawled along again and again in a manic fashion. He moved up and down hard surfaces until his knees were raw. Rather than being fascinated by whole cars or trucks, he was intensely attracted to their wheels, which he could spin for long periods with his middle finger. He did not point to indicate his needs, nor did he use toys in a functional manner. He also had moments of "spacy-ness" where he stopped all movement, staring off for seconds before resuming any movement. His preoccupations regularly interfered with his interactions with others, yet when not preoccupied he could be warm and related for brief periods. This was especially true with his mom and dad, with whom he would give wide grins and sparkly eyes when they connected. Although Graham had many features of autism, the fact that he could relate and interact, albeit briefly, meant that he did not exactly fit into an autism spectrum category. Rather, he had a severe sensory processing challenge that was affecting his social communication. An "Autistic-like" profile (also known as sensory processing disorder) is much less recognized by service providers, therefore Jennie and Erik had to deal with another layer of ambiguity and confusion trying to get all the needed services and financing to provide Graham what he needed.

New concerns often arise that require parents to sometimes devote the majority of their time and finances to help their child be the best he can be. Of course this vigilance can take a toll. Parents often do not take the time to reflect, share and resolve the myriad of emotional feelings they too are experiencing. I find this to be especially true and worrisome when parents can't find time to share with each other as is needed to keep their marriage alive.

Many parents would have been overwhelmed by all of this. Jennie and Erik became mobilized—they were like sponges soaking up all the information possible, traveling wherever to get consultation and advice, stepping up with needed enthusiasm and energy to support Graham through each challenge, including his seizures that produced the "spacey" episodes. Jennie and Erik quickly learned how to support Graham's sensory needs, which allowed them to sustain longer and longer periods of relating and communicating with him. His response was amazing. As each of his challenges, from difficulties with motor planning and visual-spatial thinking to seizures, were addressed, Graham made huge developmental progress. Today, at the age of seven he is thriving in his mainstream classes and enjoying friendships.

Both Jennie and Erik tapped into their own creativity to come to grips with their feelings as their journey with Graham progressed. Erik documented Graham's progress following early intervention services in an award-winning film. "Autistic-Like: Graham's Story" is a stunning tribute to the fortitude of their family's love for their son. By sharing their story, an uplifting hopeful message has been sent to audiences worldwide.

Jennie found her voice through expressive poetry writing. *Autism disrupted: A Mother's Journey of Hope* is a testament to the power of writing and therapeutic value of expressing one's story. In this book she welcomes us to join her through the impact and rhythm of her evocative words as she captures the emotional highs, the lows and lessons learned throughout her journey. We feel with her the initial fears, lost dreams and wrenching readjustment to a new life order that occurs following her realization of Graham's special needs. We ache with her as she yearns to be a good mother while continuing to mourn the loss of her own mother at a very young age. We cheer for her as she awakens to her own strengths, courage, and ability to handle stress. And we hope for her as she realizes that she has her own rudder to navigate the path of her life. And then we fall again with her as each new challenge for Graham reignites the old fears, disappointment and uncertainties. Ultimately we follow along with her as Graham develops, learns, gains relationships and blossoms into a charming humorous child. Her thoughts also grow and broaden to the full scope of her life as a girl, a woman, a mother, a wife—exposing old wounds, new joys, the power of healing and acceptance.

Although each child affected by autism has differing developmental growth trajectories, the emotional journey experienced by parents and family often hits similar highs and lows. Jennie captures these moments in this volume as only someone who wears these shoes can. This book will resonate with all those living and working with special needs children. It will also provide comfort to those struggling with their own feelings to know that one cannot only survive but can also find hope and peace and joy despite the pain and fear. And this then is the true value of this volume: the universality of this recurring theme. For who does not have to face challenges in their life and find themselves reaching into their mind and soul to find relevance, meaning and hope? Jennie gives this gift to all of us. When you read *Autism disrupted: A Mother's Journey of Hope* you will be so inspired and perhaps, just perhaps, will pick up pen and paper to chronicle your own unique journey! That would put a huge smile on Jennie's face!

Ricki G. Robinson, MD, MPH

Author of *Autism Solutions—*

How to Create a Healthy and Meaningful Life for Your Child

www.drrickirobinson.com

The Spirit Of Mother

—In the darkness surrounding the shining lights of my life,
I began to discern the faces of my mothers, each one
burning with her own fire.

Anita Diamant, *The Red Tent*

I watched you sweet girl
as you surrendered control
to the miracle of life.
You walked in freedom
arms swinging by your side.

I hold your hand today
as rain pours from the sky
and you, sleepy-eyed
wrapped in your white robe
are given
the gift of a lifetime.

Yes, it's true my darling girl—
there is life inside of you.
Your body is a temple,
a sacred house,
where mother Spirit
and child are born.

False Positive

The blood tests say
something may be wrong.
They crunched the numbers
into statistics,
laid them out in black and white.

They looked into the eyes
of their machines
and we watched our fetus
stretch, kick and turn
inside the home
it has made
in my womb.

It was then
he must have known
to show us who he is.

It's a boy, the nurse says,
a boy.

We will have a son.

Birth

His birth was not what I expected.
The searing contractions like flaming knives
burning through me.

The pain came fast—
every seven to fifteen minutes
it would shock me out of my skin.
I would try to run from it
until it suddenly subsided,
and then there was peace.

For five days and nights,
I laid in the bath,
walked heavily on the beach,
stopped to exhale the pain.
I prayed, meditated and pleaded
for my body, my boy,
to deliver his mother, my son.

My husband and my oldest friend
bound in loyalty and love,
stayed at my side
taking turns with sleep
to act as witness to this occasion.

I didn't want to think there was danger.
I trusted the moment
and held on to blind faith
that this labor would finally end.
In a rush,
they took him from me.

(continued)

His blue eyes found me in an instant
as my voice said his name.
Hi Graham,
Hi my Baby.

He knew me all along.

Strange Behavior

I don't know the future
behind those blue eyes—
the ones that sparkle
from the tears just shed,
blackening the thick eyelashes
he inherited from his daddy.

I see those eyes carry him
to scary places.
While on hands and knees,
he chases lines and patterns.
Back and forth,
back and forth,
on asphalt, concrete, carpet,
with shredded pant legs
and blistered hands.

Those eyes are drawn to spinning wheels.
Strollers are turned onto their side
as this fifteen month old boy
stands like a DJ entranced in joy,
as the wheels twirl in his hands.

Those eyes are windows
to a place only he knows.
A place that people out there
want to label, want to diagnose.

But it's those same eyes
that ask to play peek-a-boo,
search me out in a crowd
and recognize *me* as Mama.

Autism

Autism knocked on my door
in the middle of a life
I thought was under my control,
and settled in comfortably
behind the eyes of my two year-old son.

I am trying to get to know this condition,
to observe its daily needs,
to chart the frustrations, ecstasies,
and windows of possible change.

It swept through my house
and cleared away
all fantasies, pictures and maps
of the family
I was supposed to have.

Its luggage was heavy,
loaded with old stories,
fat with fear.

Autism leaves things lying around
ready to trip me
just as I begin to walk again.

All I Have To Be

I was told to keep it a secret—
something might be wrong
with my child.

I was told to wait for the assessments
before we exposed our fears,
exposed the nightmares
unfolding in our minds.

I could not bear to hide
the inward panic,
the fake smile
as my eyes, my heart, my body
cried to know the truth,
to share,
to be supported,
to not be so alone.

Hand in hand,
we walked into our *mommy and me* class.
I couldn't breathe.
I could feel the wall collapse
as the tears began to fall.

All eyes turned on me,
and I heard myself say,

all I ever have to be is Graham's Mom—
whoever he is,
*whatever **this** is.*
I can
and always will be
his Mom.

First Responses

I hear it in their voices,
the shaky place inside
that doesn't quite know what to say
to a mother that is facing the unbearable.

I hear the relief
drip from their forehead,
as they thank the Almighty
that this crisis did not happen to them.

Thanking the divine
that for now,
their children are spared.

I see them go about their normal days
where they watch their own children play,
and little worries come and go.

I go home to a house full of therapists
and celebrate
the simple interaction
of my son's hand in mine,

as we walk and walk,
walk away
with the unsayable diagnosis.

These Are The Rules, Autism...

Listen, autism,
I am building a room in my mind—
a place that will safely
hold you at bay.
I will be available to listen
to what you need to tell me,
but will only do so in peace.

There will be rules in this house, autism,
don't come to me with your panic and fear,
but come to me with simple information
so that I can process and understand.

Then, give me time
to know what to do.

I need space every day
to follow my own path
without autism hovering in the hallway.

My Mantra

I keep running into
that bold, fiercely courageous girl
who grew up
while her mother died around her.

She has a core of survival
that is unbreakable—
a secret place
stored away with honor.

Almost twenty years later,
she reappears
with my eyes, my heart,
my hands,
and tells me—
You can do this!

She nudges me awake at 6 a.m.
pushes me to stand up,
honor the silence,
and walk into my son's room,
expecting that this day
could hold a miracle.

I see her stand in the hallway
or wait for me in the car
simply nodding her head.

Do you remember? she says,

You can do this!

I Am Afraid

of the new woman
who grows inside of me.
Life has thrown me overboard
for six months now
into the uncharted waters called *autism*.

The storm has moved in

and hovers—
the blackness is stagnant
over my head.

I don't want to face
the loss of my old life,
or the blank slate
of my future.

The dangerous journey
has worn me thin
before I could get my feet on the ground.

I know,
I know,
I *will* walk again
on dry ground.

I just never knew
I would need to swim
so long
in deep water.

My Disappearance

I map out miracles,
creative interactions,
schedule brain scans, special meals
and blood work;
open my door to therapists at 7 a.m.,
and push my true thoughts
deeply away.

The conversations in my mind
have grown too big, too intense
for the grocery aisle
or a sandbox in the park.

In silence, I try to grasp
how to find time for my marriage
that has been placed in the wings
while our son's life
is choreographed on center stage.

My silence holds possible dreams
of a normal life—
with family vacations,
car trips, and time. . .
not just schedules.

Depression

I have become accustomed
to insurmountable stress
morning until night—
waiting for the next phone call
about my father-in-law's prognosis,
rearranging the Nanny
for bedside shifts
while he lay dying before us.

I try to hold my head up during
construction meetings for our house,
and wonder if these details
will ever matter.

I dread the constant flow of therapists,
medical exams and opinions about my son.
There is constant fear
that a sideways glance
is a seizure or a sure sign
of autistic regression.

It is my sister's concern
that finally pushes me towards help.
Miles away, I hear her voice
as I lay on my bed holding the phone.
At last, my tears finally begin to flow.

Redefining Family

I have trained myself
to stay high above the edge,
to only say that ultimately my son will be fine,
to see him through a lens of *normal*.

But, it pushes on me sometimes.
I lose my footing, and slip into the fear—
the constant work ahead
to keep him on track,
to ensure he can keep up with his peers.

I hang limp from the responsibility
and secretly weep
for the freedom of my past.

I can't trust the woman
I might become.
A river sucks me in
and I shiver in my honesty
that it will change me.

I am ashamed to reveal
that I don't have the courage
for another child,
petrified too, the weight
might pull me under.
I can't trust
that it won't happen again.

I need to control just my own life for a while
and rest,
one night's unworried sleep.

Woman In Boots

I have seen her
wearing steel-toed shit-kicking boots
ready to face the day.

Her strength has grown
and she is able to put out a stiff hand
to all the little stuff
that once sent her over the edge.

She traps life's heartaches in her chest
like a small caged bird,
gently handled with grace and wisdom.
When opened,
it carries the magic of experience
through air.

The strength has finally clung to her,
seeped into her daily life
inviting gratefulness and pride
for the little moments of a day,
and the precious heart of
this small family at home.

Christmastime

And now it is Christmastime.

It is more bittersweet this year
as if it could be taken away
so violently by hatred's hands,
or the cruel fate
of nature's fury.

I think of the mothers and fathers
sent away to war
to protect a country
that hates their presence.

I think of the letters and packages
that arrive, to give them a sense of home.

I see houses destroyed,
families forced to move,
never to return home.

I listen more closely
to the words of holiday songs on the radio,
and drive a little slower
past the houses lit with hope and joy.

I want to nestle into this season,
and surround my son with the true meaning
of this Christ Consciousness—
the celebration of kindness, giving and hope.

I see innocence in my son's small face
and the love he has for each living thing.

These special children
embody angelic minds.

He is teaching me a lot this year,
how to gather Faith in the Spirit
that leads us, down the path of our lives.

The Blue Blanket

The blue blanket
was there for it all.

I grabbed it from my son's crib
as we headed out the door,
handed it to him in the car seat,
watched as his eyes opened in delight.

His fingers wrapped around it in pieces
rubbing each side,
as if he could capture in motion
the nervous flickers in my mind.

The blanket was dragged across the office floor,
shown to the clinicians with pride
while they prepared the glue
that would attach the electrodes to his head.

I admire the bond between blanket and boy,
to know that the sight, smell, and touch of one piece of fabric
could bring about such safety.

That night,
I lay by his crib while he slept,
his head wrapped like a mummy
while a machine captured the motion in his brain.

I watched how this boy of mine
shifted about, half-dreaming
yet always holding one hand
on that precious blue cloth.

Magicians

New teachers and therapists
keep appearing in our lives,
ready and eager to encourage my son
to grow on the developmental ladder.

I see the determination in their eyes
and I feel like a lost little girl,
as I lie at their feet
praying for miracles.

Will one get him to jump?
Will another get him to use his hands?

Sometimes, one will speak of the future,
as they try to calm my fears.

He may never write with his hands,
but technology has come so far.

He will find his special place in the world.

I know there is truth in those words,
but then I have to crawl away from their feet
and stand alone
realizing
there is no magic teacher
that will make it all disappear.

It Slides Under The Door

I am cloaked in that old fear again.
It started at a parent teacher conference.

I could feel it slide under the door
as we settled into our conference chairs,
placed our papers on a table.

The teacher started the meeting somberly,
I want to tell you,
I saw Graham have a seizure yesterday.

The fog swirled around my breath.

The hope of my son
going off the epileptic medication
broke into jagged shards
of sadness.

Love Poem

I want to write a love poem
for the mother I am today.

I want to tell her it's okay to have those days
when it hurts
as in the park today,
when she watched another three-year-old boy
move his body with ease,
his parents unaware
of brainpower the body must use
to accomplish such tasks.

I want to write a love poem to this mother
who is the very light in her son's eyes.

I want her to notice how he leans his body closer to her lap,
one arm always attached,
held on to, protected.

I want her to witness the bond of mother to son,
to witness the perfection
of just that simple thing.

I want her to know that no one in this world
can alter, judge, assess, label,
or destroy that miracle.

I want to write a love poem to this mother
who sits in a chair tonight,
tired and frustrated.

(continued)

I want her to remember these moments with clarity, to remember that each day comes and goes.

To remember that the big things and little things have turned out okay.

Turning Thirty-Five

My search for grace
has become more narrowed with age.

I have for decades
researched and collected women of all ages
to dissect, define and map out
the pathways of a woman's journey.
I want them to show me
how a motherless daughter
navigates the role of wife, friend, mother, and sister.

I am moving toward thirty-five;
A number that seems crucial,
more stable, heavier in confidence,
not so easily swayed by passing winds.
Age holds more experience,
more cycles that have finally reached the point of exhaustion
and been forced to change.

I guess it means
I have finally collected enough from my own life,
to begin to trust myself as the guide.

My Husband, Lover, and Friend

—for Erik

His pace is more sure now.
He has stopped running into crowds of expectations,
waving frantically
many masks
of proven success.

His stride is determined
as if the path of authenticity
opened its doors
and paved a clean road,
driven with honesty, and personal vision.

He became a warrior before my eyes—
fatherhood cloaking him in purpose
and an immense desire to share his journey.

He said, *Yes*
in a deep exhale,
Yes, to all that was within him.

I have watched in admiration
as the man I love
walked through the heavy muck of life,
the death of his father,
the diagnosis of his only child.

Through faith, we crossed over
the dangerous line where most marriages crumble
under the weight of grief.
Somewhere amongst the minutes and the hours,
we walked into a new light.
I sleep beside this man.

New Picture

I see a new picture.
It appears as a little boy
with a big-boy bed,
real boy underwear on long legs.

He is coming out of a lost place
this independent boy,
self-aware,
fully emerging.

I finally see
the years melt away
into a boy
I get to meet each morning,
again and again.

I made it past darkness,
and I know it can work.

I believed, through faith,
and watched the healing unfold.

Weeks, minutes,
it all adds up.
Scheduled time reveals
and shares its growth.

Children emerge,
boys become boys.

Tennessee Waits For Me

Tennessee has waited for over a year
to open her sweet, plump arms
and take me home again.

This time,
she will embrace my son,
envelop him
in her sticky,
vibrant air of summer.

A mother and her son
on our first adventure.

This place of my childhood
will be seen
through his excited eyes.

Stories of fireflies
that sparkle as the hot sun
dims to dusk—
sweet moments
just before darkness.

The symphony of cicadas in trees
will begin their crescendo,
the finale of our long days.

I will see his chubby hands
reach into a flowing pond
looking for frogs
hidden in rocks,
the croak, and plop
at the slightest sound.

We will drive down a country road,
take a breath of sweet air.

Fill me up,
my Southern home,

fill him up.
Give him this piece of me
to share, to love.

The Zoo

I remember it was hot,
sticky, humid-hot
where air above the asphalt parking lot
quivered, blurred my vision.
Expectations hovered
over me as I watched
my dad and son
climb from the car.
This was my hometown zoo.

Scanning the surroundings,
I was desperate for memories of this place
where my little feet once
traveled amongst the wonders
of animals.

I unlatched the trunk.
A strange ache settled between my shoulders,
the dread of disappointment yet to come
in the hours ahead.
I didn't want to need the stroller,
but I knew it was necessary.

I brushed off the sadness,
like swatting a fly from my face.
Moms do that you know,
move forward,
and just hold their breath
along the way.

The child in me
stood at the ticket counter,

pigtails in her hair,
physically bouncing
with anticipation.

I wanted to share
the mystery of wild animals with my son,
to have him stare into their eyes for a moment.

The heat felt blinding
as an ache from within said,
at least your son will appear normal
as he sits in the stroller.

The path turned,
my dad and I stopped in our amazement
as the massive elephants
came into view.

There they were—
right in front of us—
no crowd to hide our view.
Their long, wrinkled, smelly trunks
snorting up cool, dark water,
and throwing it backwards
into the air
spraying their giant backs
in sheer delight.

(continued)

It filled me like caffeine,
a rush to share
this perfect performance
with my two-year-old son.

I scooped him out of the stroller
and held him high,
perched him on a wooden railing.

He scrambled in my arms,
struggled and kicked
to be let free.
His eyes,
his joy,
his will,
like a laser beam
down to the stroller,
down to the hot ground,
down to the finite motion
of a wheel
making contact with the ground.

Autism Disrupted

*—When the sensory system is severely enough affected
to derail relating and communicating,
then you are headed down the autistic spectrum pathway.*
Dr. Stanley Greenspan
Founder of DIR/Floortime

Dr. Greenspan's words
settle down next to my anxiety,
and with a knowing hand,
gently push aside my panic and confusion
with clear explanations
about my son's development.

Graham's obsessions with lines, wheels,
and the sturdiness of a hard floor
brought comfort to our boy
whose sensory system could not regulate
the chaos of his world.

Our miracle awaited us in a playroom—
carefully constructed
like a microcosm of our larger world,
with designated areas,
labeled and free of distractions,
used to rebuild neuro-pathways through play.
With toys that he loved,
games were created to motivate
imagination, circles of communication,
and motor planning of his body.

(continued)

Therapist after therapist
arrived at our door
holding their bags of tricks—
and the magic of play.

In our home, this playroom
at the bottom of our stairs,
became an entryway to emotion and interaction.
A world of relationships opened its door to Graham,
and the door of autism
closed behind him.

Remember This My Son

The world will always
push you to accomplish more.
With every age,
comes expectations,
and the bar gets raised a little higher.

I see the teachers with their charts.
They watch to see
if you can write your name,
know your letters,
understand the logic of math.

I want you to know
that in *your* home,
the bar stays the same.

You can step through our door
every day of your growing years,
and know that we love and accept you
as you are this day.

The key to the kingdom
is love and acceptance.
If I can leave you
with *that* legacy,
you will realize
that home is always
inside of you.

Ashes

My six-year-old son looks up at me
with a toothless smile.
His eyes are eager
for the history of this mysterious place—
Captiva Island.

We pedal our bikes past
the land where my grandfather's house once stood.
I watch myself in the video of my mind,
a little girl fishing off the dock,
boat rides to Useppa Island,
the peeling skin of sunburns,
the toothy laughter
with a family that no longer exists.

That house was destroyed by a hurricane.
My grandparents' ashes have been scattered in the Bay.

All of my family gone,
how they loved this island.
I stand in their history.

On our bikes,
I mention the historic cemetery
at the Chapel By The Sea.
My son's long legs pedal faster,
eager to see the headstones.
His chatter busy over ideas
of bodies buried underground,
or scattered in places loved.

Our feet shuffle
through the sandy graveyard
as he says to me,
Don't worry Mama,
we will sprinkle your ashes here too someday,
and then he skips away.

Graduation

—Letter to the staff at Smart Start Preschool

This school, the staff,
have altered a life,
blessed my baby into a boy.

The foundations of his life
have been built
with your hands.

Through years of navigation—
endless hours
of therapeutic play,

he was given the gift
of problem-solving
to replace tantrums.
His isolation
opened into friendship,
his anxiety to confidence,
apprehension to joy.

I have to say good-bye,
and there is a deep ache inside my body
mixed with grief.
I weep with gratitude.

From the holiest
of places inside,
I say *thank you.*

Thank you.

Welcome to Kindergarten

A new big boy school,
with a fast-paced plan.
The staff was ready—
to test, evaluate
and expose his disability.
Ready to pounce like tigers,
on the weakest.

The pressure began on day one—
write your name,
do your homework,
cut and glue!

The weight of expectations,
twenty-one kids and a teacher
who could not slow down.

I shook
as I sent him walking into room 1
with his green monogrammed backpack
hanging heavily on his fragile frame.

The tantrums of frustration
started again,
saved up during the school day.
This transition became a war zone at home
of hitting, spitting, and tears,
as his heart screamed
for safety, security, success.

(continued)

He is my mirror—
the war raged in me as well.
Peace and flow of our house crumbled

I was buried under new assessments,
days of charted tests
from school psychologists, speech therapist, and
special education teacher.
Multiple IEP meetings were scheduled,
stuffed in an early morning conference room
where I silently bit back the devastation
of being told he would need an aide.

Broken again,
I shielded daggered glances and comments
from parents in the classroom
as they watched him struggle to write.
Didn't your son go to preschool?
I nodded my head, yes,
the story too long to retell.

The Rush of Life

has swept us,
my husband and me
away from each other.

We wake early,
push through our days,
drag loaded carts of
deadlines, duties and destinations,
dump them
at the end of the day
as we hurry home
for a family meal,
homework, bath, and bedtime stories.

As I close my son's bedroom door,
my body aches for silence.
There is nothing left to give.

The White Notebook

The white notebook
travels through my son's days
nestled in his green backpack
hiding secret observations,
his moment to moment victories,
suggestions of topics to be discussed,
and activities
I never hear about
at the family dinner.

Some days
his aide holds the key
to a dusty, dark box
of wounded memories—
a fragile place inside me
I thought was locked away.

Her words, *he seemed off today,*
unable to focus,
crack the lid a little wider.

I try to breathe
as I read daily reports,
knowing that the peace I long for
in these moments
will never be found in the dark.

Standing Tall

I watch my son Graham in therapy
move his body.
The light of success in his face,
the sound of his laughter,
as new connections fire in his brain.

I watch myself lean
against the wall of the therapy room,
crouched, arms tight around my knees,
scared, hopeful, holding shame
and the secret judgments
of a life I sometimes feel went wrong.

I see my eyes in the reflection of the mirrored wall—
they dance or drop
depending on Graham's progress that day.

This feeling is familiar.
My eyes have risen and fallen
a thousand times as I watch my son.

I want to try a different path,
smoother, on a more neutral plane,
where I can step out
of the role of mother
and see a woman,
myself, standing tall,
walking in and out of the moments in her day.

She knows that nothing needs to be fixed.
Nothing needs to be different
than it is right now.

Welcome to First Grade

My son now goes to first grade.
At 8 a.m. he disappears
into Grandview Elementary School
hidden on the side of a hill.
I release him to his big boy world
until the afternoon.

The heavy ache,
the stone that used to sit in my belly
during Kindergarten, has softened.

There is a new faith in the school,
an ever-growing faith in my Graham.

This boy who just completed
his first spelling test,
who writes his name,
and proudly yells out the sight words on the flashcards.
Why, he can chase a soccer ball down the field.

It was once said,
he might never get this far.

Autism disrupted: *A Mother's Journey of Hope*

On the Sidelines

I stand on the sidelines of the soccer field—
fold-up chairs, water bottles, snack wrappers,
filled with energy for the game.

I dreamed of this moment,
to stand in the league of typical parenthood
where boys just play soccer
because that is what you do in Fall.
Saturdays are spent at the field
where we watch and gossip
while our boys run back and forth—
an amoeba of bodies chasing a ball.

There are so many untold stories
masked on these sidelines—
a Dad who forgot the red jersey
because he doesn't communicate with his ex-wife.
They sit across the field from each other,
an unspoken energy between them.

A mother, who after mindless chatter,
casually mentions
she just recovered from lung cancer.

And, there is me,
a Mom who holds her breath
every time her son touches the ball.
A mother who is still told to check
the box of autism on medical forms
to ensure attention for her son.

(continued)

She secretly praises his progress
but stays wary just in case.

Who is this boy
who joyfully bounds through the green grass
looking like the other *normal* boys?

And who is this Mom
that hides her story?
Years of therapy, medication and doctors—
stuffed in her pocket
as she sits back, silent, in a folded chair
pretending this is where she should be.

Moments I Can't Protect Him From

He is now in that stage, I think,
where memories get stored.
When my son is older,
he will rummage around
in the warehouse of childhood moments:
first smooth rides on his red-flamed bicycle,
Santa's magic footprint on Christmas mornings,
campfire skits, midnight snacks,
sleeping bag snuggles camping with his dad.
But, I wonder what the disappointing memories will be,
or the first recollections of fear.

I awoke yesterday
to the sound of his screams.
My independent boy
had gotten up quietly,
went down in the basement to play.
I found him shrieking,
his tall lanky body shook with tears.
A large spider had crawled from a new toy box,
and terrorized his solitude.
Where is that memory stored in his Psyche—
the moments I can't protect him from:
spiders, unkind words, judgments,
and scenes of an inconsistent world.

Put Your Hands to Rest

Hey now,
hey now,
be gentle with yourself—
mothers of this special world.

You too, are special—
chosen to make peace
with this uncharted path.

Put your busy hands to rest.
Tell the nagging critic to step aside.
You have done enough for today,
guilt moves you nowhere.

Go inside, dear one,
where labels don't matter.

Stop!
Did you hear me?
Stop!

Wrap your arms around yourself
and say out loud:

I am enough,
I Am Enough,
TODAY.

Consequences of Silence

The little girl inside me still walks around
with her head held high,
parading ribbon-barrettes
that drape her smooth blonde hair.

She stuffed down what she should have said,
pushed what she needed into her pink backpack,
crammed her feelings into bags of leotards,
painted over her pain
with stage makeup.

She excelled at cover-up,
a soloist dancer
whose mother had died in the wings.

Today, she drops the curtain,
reveals the imperfections,
and withdraws from the performance.

Her body listened,
even if she did not,
her voice was silent—
surgeries were needed,
wounds did not close,
doctors were baffled—
hernias tore on the inside.

She learned her body
cannot heal when she doesn't speak.

Snowbound

I have been snowbound.
My body, beaten by storms of surgeries and pain,
has kept me underground.

The blizzard of early parenthood
is finally dying down,
no longer does it whip me
with diagnosis and fear.

It has been a time of healing—
forced to be confined,
forced to stop.

My mind looks inward—
shuffles around in the cold, snowy silence,
uncovering sadness, false beliefs,
hidden safely beneath the weight
of white snow.

I feel warmth
of a new sun—
burn, shine, melt,
the heavy places.

Time for me to come out.
Time for me to share my light.

Mistakes

I hear my mistakes—
those moments when I walk away
and something seems to follow me.

They stick to my breath,
stop me in a daze,
and urge me to find resolution.

It happens when I lose my temper
with our son,
or lash out in defensiveness
to a casual comment from my husband.

The mistake lingers
with shame and disappointment,
like a rotten smell you just can't find in the kitchen.

An apology is never enough—
it's so much heavier than that.

Do No Harm

A woman appears in my backyard—
her face tipped to the sky,
her arms hang down,
palms open.
She is silent,
and her eyes are closed.

I stand on the second floor balcony,
lean into an iron rail.
Oh, there is blood on my hands
from my inner battle
with whips and chains.

I was a terrible mom today, I say,
I pushed him too hard.

My wounds of guilt
ooze with failed expectations for my son.
I am heavy with shame in my disappointment,
and lack of approval
in these moments of my motherhood.

I bow my head in defeat.
The woman raises her arms to me,
and I want to walk into her embrace,
to hear her say,
It's okay,
it's okay sweet girl.
You are not these things.
Now forgive yourself,
and do no more harm.

I Am Willing

There is a place of willingness in me,
to look again
through the door
opened by my frantic, fear-filled critic,
asking me
to step inside
the tornado of churning thoughts.

I ask this stormy, scared self,
What is it
that needs to be heard, to be healed?

Fear it says, the paralyzing fear.
Take a good look through this door.
It DOES NOT serve you!
Why do you keep coming back here?

Walk the other way.

I Belong

I have lived among excuses—
gathered them around me like blankets
to cover and protect
the bright light
of who I am.

It's just a home we built.

       I just used an old recipe.

I'm just a regular ol' mom.

       Those surgeries were no big deal.

I just dabble in poetry.

I wonder why I hid.
Minimized my innate gifts.
Hidden the great expressions of Spirit in my life.

I get spooked sometimes
when I dare myself to see my life.
To see the beauty, feel the joy
of a life manifested before me.

A warm, loving, beautiful home,
a tender, wise partner,
a man who has chosen me
to walk with for his lifetime.

The miracle of a son
who is growing up amongst us—
school nights, birthday parties,
dinners, trips, tears and time—
so much time.

I have a family.
I am a mother, wife, poet, therapist, student,
friend, sister, daughter.

I am a temple of life.
I belong.

I Promised Him A Different Afternoon

I had   promised him
the night before
to do something   crazy
to celebrate the 100th day of school.
Promised him
an afterschool play date with Mom,
no homework,
an afternoon
different   than before,
different   than our usual routine.

His eyes bore into me,
pulling   on my pant leg
as I signed him out of school.

The lights of the arcade
flashed   from the parking lot.
Remember,
I   promised him   crazy.
Remember,
I   promised him   different.
The usual parents
were   locked
into their cell phones,
handing out tokens
from their   busy   hands.
I set my bag down
and slid tokens
into both slots,
took my place at his side,
my own   superhero character
steering the snowmobile

through treacherous mountains,
my own   set of balls
flinging into the numbered holes
behind the glass machine,
toy tickets
flooding out of the dispenser,
Let's do this one Mama!
Look, I won Mama!
as we cheered,
high-fived,
and fist bumped
our way through the maze of machines.

I was   feverish
with the joy of adrenaline
that pumped through me.
Young girls in uniforms
glanced my way,
staring at the mother
as she squealed,
giggled, screamed with her son.

I caught the wave of crazy,
saw the pride in his eyes.
His mama was   different,
she   played,
she   promised,

and the whole world
was brighter for a day.

Old and New Stones

They are really quite simple, you know,
these pieces of jewelry
I put on and take off every day.
But, there is great meaning underneath
the multi-faceted worn stones
that travel with me throughout my days.
Jewels that have adorned
the women of my ancestry.

I slip their rings onto my fingers—
my mom, and my grandmother.
They sit on my fingers
and hold the broken places inside
that ache for the wisdom
of their complicated legacy.

A thin silver chain supports a circle of tiny diamonds,
as it rests above my heart with it's own story to tell.
It's my love story—
the one I never thought I was worthy of.
This man who chose me as his wife
took me away on a treasure hunt
to all the places of our past—
magical spots in the alleys of San Francisco
where our story began.

My husband, whose eyes
have been passed on to our son
reached across a table
and handed me a box.

This is for you, Jennie—
I celebrate you as my wife, as a mother.

Even now, I touch my neck sometimes,
rub the circle of stones with my finger.
I breathe in awe of its fragility—
my life, my marriage,
my story.

Horizons

It has been thirteen years since the moment we stood
on the roof of my flat in San Francisco
tasting that new sweet salt
of lips, tongues, and hands.
The horizons of young love
settled into the fog of a night.

Under a white tent along the Tennessee River,
I made promises of *new* horizons—
till death do us part, in sickness and in health,
bound by the ceremonial contract to God.

Our guests were there to witness.
They were supposed to remind us,
nurture our marriage, and hold our hands
as we crossed the rocky roads
and unknown paths of our future.

But, it comes to me now,
I too often forget
the vow of kindness I made to him.
The promises of new horizons,
of peace, care, and tenderness in our home.

Our guests aren't here to remind me,
and, guilt keeps tapping on my shoulder.

Autism disrupted: *A Mother's Journey of Hope*

Let Me Walk With You

Let me walk with you my Love.
Allow me to walk in the rawness
of my vulnerability.

Today, I need only to know
that you can hold this shaken space
within me right now,
and not pick at it, judge it,
or try to fix it.

Today, I need you to reach out
and take my hand,
wrap your arms around me,
stand in this moment with me
to actually *feel* my discomfort.

Then, my dear Love,
I promise,
I will uncover
the confusion, the inner angst
that pull me away from you.

Patterns Paused

I hold my responsibility
heavy in my hand tonight,
resolute to own my part
in our marriage's rusty performance.

I have been the starring role—
an overwhelmed heroine
who cries out to my hero
to fix small dramas in my days.

Oh, but let me tell you,
the martyr inside me
makes me mean,
lashing out against his kindness.

The rage is my solo—
a self-monologue
of judgment, over pleasing,
and old beliefs of unworthiness.

Finally broken,
I throw down the tattered script.

The audience no longer fills the velvet seats,
our finale has fallen flat.
Drama doesn't work anymore.

I must stand
in the ambiguity of life,
be in the not knowing,
and stop pushing and pulling—
daggered projections of self-doubt
onto the one man
who has never wavered.

We Are Listening

There are two wise women
who walk behind me always.
I envision them holding hands
and I think I have heard the hymn of a gospel song.
Warmly, they place their hands on my back, smiling.
This is love in action,
as they pour sweetness over me like sugar.

These women of the Divine walk tall,
long silver hair flows freely in the breeze.
They watch me,
so finely tuned to all the shifts in my daily thoughts—
jolts in the equilibrium of peace.

One nudges the other with her elbow.
It is time, she says.

The other woman, my muse,
places my hands into the depths of honesty,
and puts my pen to paper,
to capture the universal shift in consciousness—
our learning moments of being human.

They go with me and sit silently by my side.
Yes, they say,
Yes, sweet girl,
write the unspoken truths—
the moments of our mortal sisterhood.

Burn

Morning, in my kitchen,
ceramic coffee cups,
Los Angeles Times,
questions of cereal or oatmeal,
the buzzing of a blender,
louder than I can bear,
please, please,
emulsify the raw powder,
frozen fruit and soy milk quickly,
so that they will fuel and nourish my body.
One cup of coffee,
in the dark,
a few minutes
of *The Today Show* by myself.
Stuff sandwiches
and savory snacks
into my son's lunchbox,
search for his shoes,
and we are out the door
to climb the short hill to school.
Back at home,
the flash of steamy water,
a pounding heat on my back,
wash, wash, clear
out for my day.

(continued)

A click of lights,
and my office shines.
I reach for the matchbox,
strike the flame
and fire sputters
on the black wick of my candle,
grey smoke of fragile beginnings
travel into air.

Light my way, I say,
keep the flame fertile,
free the expressions I touch today.
Guide me, through these precious hours.
Burn with me,
inspire me,
burn.

I Can Go Back There

Golden moments are
captured in carved picture frames
scattered amongst books, magazines,
pens, coffee cups, and clutter.
Two lives in motion.
I stare out from our photograph.
I can go back there
in my body.
Each cell remembers
the draped wedding veil
as it brushed against my bare back.
My lean, tan arms
gripped his strong forearm.
It seemed my whole body leaned in,
filled with pride
as he spoke vows to me.
It was June.
The afternoon sun
looked like fire
in the trees behind us.
The black-and-white photo
doesn't show the rich colors of that day
now left to the energy of imagination.
I'm telling you, the color was brilliant,
and I, I was immersed in the presence
of his words.
My face radiated
with his promises.
My sweet Love,
My sweet, sweet Love—
you have loved me for so long.

Solitude

Two hours left
of precious solitude
before the   rush
of my son's little feet
runs through the door,
and demands all of me.

Stories burst
from his well of memory.
Mama!   he will yell
as he crosses the threshold,
his karate bag,
backpack,
Scooby-Doo lunchbox, in tow.

And I will be ready
to hold his day in my hands.
Ready, to anchor and ground
possible tears and tantrums
as the day's sensory storm
settles, transitions into night.

But for now, right now,
our cats follow me
from room to room
as I search
for my pen, my notebook.

They know I will stop,
snuggle in,
nourish myself
in our   silence.

Laughter

The slight   giggle
caught by the wind,
covering our faces
in the fancy restaurant,
like little kids,
like we were   once
in our twenties.
He catches his laughter
in his hand,
covering his beard,
his bright blue eyes
caught like a   secret.
He truly thinks I am funny,
says he wishes sometimes
there was someone beside him
to witness my expressions,
the innocent-isms
that flow out of me
only to him.
I feel like we are   falling again,
falling   into the love
of the adults we have become,
so many   stories,
so many   moments
from our creative days,
caught like a net,
when you really   stop,
really   stop
to listen,
like best friends
trying to catch up,
trying to fill
the need to   know,
to laugh,
to care.

Please

I am depleted
of all energy to engage.

I smile
at the high-pitched,
joyful voices of Graham and his dad
as they play toy soldiers in battle.

Please,
let me just revel in this moment.
Please,
push away the heaviness
I have carried
inside of me these past days.

Heaviness,
that needed my son
to go back to school,
heaviness,
that just longed for solitude.
I am finished
for the moment
with my seven-year-old's raging independence.

I am done with constant defiance.
Done, too, with talking down of tantrums
over the simplest requests.

Please,
don't let my husband and son
see me like this.

Please,
allow me to close the door
and wake up to a new day.

The Weight of Generations

The past five days
stretch out like a movie,
a movie I have longed to play a part in,
sisters unraveling
threads of our common history.

We sit on the floor,
deep into dusty boxes,
amongst piles of yellowed journals
written in multiple languages,
letters postmarked from Paris and Brussels,
eloquently reveal the voice
of our grandmother—
the writer, the poet, the regal bohemian
who mixed among royalty.
We learn about her life as a widow
and as a renegade activist
living in the South.
Stories of marches with Martin Luther King,
crosses burned outside her window,
and memories of being protected
by the National Guard.

Her daughter, our mother,
grew up amongst the heroes of that time,
shadowed by the grandiosity around her.
Letters uncover
her tragic history,
the life cut short by cancer,
leaving her own children
to dig for answers.

(continued)

Two motherless daughters,
holding in our hands
the weight of generations—
and the secret mixed misinterpretations
on how to be a woman,
a lover,
a wife,
an intellect,
a writer,
a mother.

I Can't Stop Thinking About My Father

the one consistent man
who kept a steady, successful pace
among the passionate swings—
the fame filled highs,
and desperate lows
of the matriarchs
who captured his love.

Somehow,
homework got done,
dinners got made,
and his two daughters
reached adulthood.

Somehow,
this uncomplicated man
became the beacon
of a life I want to lead—
meaningful work,
dinner at seven,
and a partner
who has adored him
for over twenty years,
always at his side.

Acceptance

Something shifted this past year,
a settling down in my soul.
My thoughts are not exclamation points anymore.
It seems easier to breathe,
and have a peaceful patience for what is yet to come.

I see that I am not the one in charge
of the world as it spins around me.

It is not my responsibility
to change my son's future path,
to make my husband's career a success,
to prove my worthiness
to this world.

I can only control
the peace and pace of my days.

I love the saying
that every person is doing the best they can
right now with the sensibility and belief systems
they have in place at the present moment.

I was always able to feel
compassion and empathy
toward others.

Finally,
I experiment with them
on myself.

I Want To Capture The Light

This day feels light, like the sun.
I want to capture this light,
trap it in velvet curtains,
stitched, embroidered
with rich reds, golds and yellows,
draped over every room,
that warms my blood—
with an invitation
to snuggle, nestle in,
to the coziness of my life.

This morning, a smile is on my son's face
as he says *thank you, I love you.*
Pride simmers perfectly
inside a pot of parenting.
We have a new recipe in motion—
a feast prepared
to feed on positive discipline.

New systems in place
to taste the sweetness of respect,
smooth swallow of politeness,
the satisfaction
of rules made with love.
I open my arms to receive it,
even just for this one day.

There is a New Voice

Some of the joy
has come back to me.
A different voice from within
has walked out of the trenches,
and I have begun to wipe the sweat off my brow.

Our family
has stepped into a new home
that has deep roots
and a long future.

The small song of hope
rises in me—
the strength of a mother's love
for a child that is beating the odds.

I have earned this pride
through hours of trainings,
days spent down on the floor
on hands and knees
playing one on one
and praising the simplest task
of one block stacked onto another,
a puzzle piece placed in the right spot.
There are words, so many words
that explode from my son's mouth.

I smile on the inside knowing
that life is awesome
in its challenges,
knowing that the maps lead us
to new places
that hold the best for us,
the best me I never knew I could be.

Autism disrupted: *A Mother's Journey of Hope*

Ease

I don't want to forget or abandon
the power and passion
of my core
that wants to do it all.

It is those layers of love
that have grown roots
into myself
over decades of time.

Yet, I want to discard
that rough broken branch
fueled by anxiety and fear,
dreams and heavy days
darkened with splinters of self-judgment.

I fed judgments with fear
believing it would strengthen me,
protect me,
and motivate growth.

I see now
that it stunted me,
held me in a place
where I could not see the sun.

It's hard to describe the change.
It is smoother now,
growth not constantly snagged,
picked on, measured.
It is growth with ease.

Now,
I can see the far side
of the line of trees.

The Secret

I get it,
the only life I can truly save
is my own.

I am guilty, and wanted
to put the responsibility on others,
to drag my husband
into the depths of my victimhood.

It was too hard
to think that I was the dark-colored thread
always woven
into the gray days of my life.

I see that the dark thread
can be unraveled,
piece by piece,
into intelligible reasons
of how I take care of myself.

I can change the color.
I can save my life.

I Wasn't Surprised

that it would be me,
out of all the other moms I knew,
to come face to face with the world of
autism, seizures and sensory disorders.

This journey has led me
down a unique path
that has forever altered my views
on children, development, parenthood,
the environment, our world
and the definition of a good family.

Life has never let me
live in the mainstream.
Why then, should I be surprised
that my family may not be so typical either?

I don't know that woman
who dreamed of a perfect family.
But, I do know, and well,
the woman who persevered,
who dove into research, and faith,
who tested the core of a marriage.

I know this woman
who has seen death,
who has seen life,
who has seen a miracle in her boy.

(continued)

This woman whose heart breaks at every phone call
from a mom in fear,
grieving a new diagnosis,
can finally say
she has seen the other side,
champions early intervention,
and can rise up in hope.

I know *that* woman well,
and will trust her always.

About The Author

Jennie Chapman Linthorst is the founder of LifeSPEAKS Poetry Therapy, providing insight and guidance for people of all ages seeking an outlet through expressive writing. Jennie has facilitated poetry therapy workshops at UC Irvine Extension, the University of Santa Monica, and in retirement homes and women's centers. In addition to her workshops, Jennie works privately with individuals and parents exploring their personal histories through reading and writing poetry.

Jennie holds a BA in Psychology from Skidmore College, and has completed her certification as a Certified Applied Poetry Facilitator from the National Association of Poetry Therapy. In 2011, she received her Master's degree in Spiritual Psychology from the University of Santa Monica, emphasizing the evolution of human consciousness.

Her poetry and essays have been featured online at *Hopeful Parents, Our Journey Through Autism, WOW! Women on Writing, Sensory Flow,* and *The Gift: A Blog for Caregivers of Sensational Children,* and others.

The compelling story of her son's diagnosis of autism and sensory processing disorder, and the success with early intervention therapies is captured in the award-winning documentary film *Autistic-Like: Graham's Story.* www.autisticlike.com.

Jennie coaches clients all across the country and around the world via phone, Skype, and email, in addition to in person meetings. More information about her workshops and private practice can be found at www.lifespeakspoetrytherapy.com.

Jennie lives in Manhattan Beach, California, with her husband Erik, and their son, Graham. She is a native of Knoxville, TN.